This book belongs to:

_____

Start date:

_____

calm
YOUR ANXIETY

60 biblical quotes for better mental health

Other Books by Robert J. Morgan

calm
YOUR ANXIETY

60 biblical quotes for better mental health

ROBERT J. MORGAN

W PUBLISHING GROUP

AN IMPRINT OF THOMAS NELSON

Introduction

I've been robbed many times, and it's no fun! Sometimes the creep enters through the front door; sometimes he breaks a back window; once he cut a hole in the roof. On every occasion, he's after only one thing—my peace of mind, the calmness I need to function in life.

His name is Anxiety, and he's a killer. He wants me to worry myself to death.

He's plying his wicked trade against millions and billions of people, for the world is more anxious than it's ever been. Pandemics and politics have made things worse. Wars and rumors of wars put the whole earth on edge. Personal problems and family issues can worry us to the point of wanting to die. Our whole world is being plundered by fear in its many forms.

Thanks be to God, I've increasingly learned to thwart this hideous villain. Doctors and counselors have helped. Friends and family have been invaluable. But by far my best defense is the Book I hold in my hand and the God who gave it to me.

The Bible is packed with chapters, verses, truths, promises, commands, and antidotes to worry and anxiety. Each sentence is a sharp weapon against the Enemy, a two-edged sword (Hebrews 4:12).

In my fight against worry, I've chosen a biblical hero—Eleazar ben Dodo—as a model. He was one of David's mighty warriors who fought the Enemy with such relentless force that after the battle his hand was frozen to his sword and his men had to help him pry it from his grasp (2 Samuel 23:9–10).

We have God's Word as a sword, and as long as we wield it in the power of God's Spirit and in the name of God's Son, Jesus, we'll be "safe and secure from all alarm." The devil attacks us with anxiety, but he cannot penetrate the defenses provided by the God who never worries, who controls time and eternity, and who works all things for our good (Romans 8:28).

So don't give up! Not ever! You can usher Archenemy Anxiety to the door, throw him out, lock the bolt behind him, and do as Scripture says: "Be careful, keep calm and don't be afraid. Do not lose heart" (Isaiah 7:4).

I believe the Bible is the best self-help Book ever written because it's our God-helps-us Book. Among its many passages on inner peace, three are classic anti-anxiety passages I've memorized:

- Psalm 37:1–8, where David said, "Do not fret."
- Matthew 6:25–34, where Jesus said, "Do not worry."

- Philippians 4:4–9, where Paul said, "Do not be anxious about anything."

In *Calm Your Anxiety: 60 Biblical Quotes for Better Mental Health*, I focus on the latter, knowing that millions of people claim Philippians 4:6 as their favorite verse of all: "Do not be anxious about anything, but in every situation, by prayer and petition, with thanksgiving, present your requests to God."

We're told if we follow the strategy of Philippians 4:4–9, the peace of God will rule our minds and hearts—and the God of peace will be with us.

That's His promise. That's our reality.

I want to suggest you spend two months—60 days—looking carefully into these verses with me. Each day's reading is short, biblical, and practical. In the process, our gracious God will enable you to calm your anxiety with divine words inspired by Him who also calmed the raging sea (Matthew 8:26).

As you read each day's portion, ask God to make it real to you. Look up the verse references in your own Bible. If you don't have a Bible, this is a great time to acquire one. Use this book like a manual for installing a personal security system around your heart.

Jesus said, "The thief comes only to steal and kill and destroy; I have come that they might have life, and have it to the full" (John 10:10). When it comes to anxiety, it's time to throw the rascal out and let our Lord's abundant life fill our hearts and minds.

God's peace is higher than earth's problems.

His calm is deeper than our chaos.

His mercy is wider, like the wideness of the sea.

He can help you cope with these anxious times and live in the calm assurance of His overwatching care. As Exodus 14:14 says: "The LORD himself will fight for you. Just stay calm" (NLT).

Thank you for picking up this daily reader. Please consider sharing it with a friend or using it in your study group. And let me end with one of the Bible's great blessings:

Now may the Lord of peace himself give you peace
. . . at all times
and in every way.
The Lord be with all of you.
2 THESSALONIANS 3:16

I will be filled with joy because of you. I will sing praises to your name, O Most High.
PSALM 9:2 NLT

Several years ago, a religious teacher in India named Meher Baba gained a global audience with his odd brand of Eastern mysticism. His most famous saying was short and simple: "Don't worry. Be happy." In America, Baba's message struck a chord with aging baby boomers and coming-of-age Gen Xers. One of his devotees, Bobby McFerrin, turned Baba's slogan into a popular 1980s song: "Don't Worry, Be Happy." McFerrin sang in a breezy style with a playful Caribbean accent and dubbed in the instrumental parts with sounds made with his voice.

If only it were that easy!

Imagine! What if a four-word slogan could transport us to a Caribbean beach with no shirt, no shoes, and no problems? If only a mantra could produce a life of cool drinks, lapping waters, tropical breezes, and orange sunsets.

But life isn't an illusion and worry cannot be managed so easily. It takes more than four words of a song. It takes the fourth chapter of Philippians and the solid truths it contains. The slogan "Don't worry, be happy" may express the reality we want, but it provides no road map for getting there. It has no compass. It has no doctrine and no theology. It has no foundation in reality. It has pep all right, but no promise.

The Bible says little about being happy, because happiness is an emotion that comes and goes depending on happenings. The Bible speaks of something deeper—joy and rejoicing, which are dispositions of the heart. That's why joy and sorrow are not mutually exclusive. Jesus was anointed with the oil of joy, yet He wept (Hebrews 1:9; John 11:35). The apostle Paul spoke of being sorrowful, yet always rejoicing (2 Corinthians 6:10).

Happiness is an emotion; joy is an attitude. Attitudes are deeper; they are richer; and the right attitudes provide the soil for healthier emotions as we mature. Emotions come and go, but attitudes come and grow. According to Philippians 4:4, the first step toward overcoming anxiety is cultivating the attitude of rejoicing.

It's not *Don't worry; be happy.*

It's *"Rejoice in the Lord always. I will say it again: Rejoice!"*

It's possible for you to be joyful today.

What adjustments can you make in your own life so you can cultivate the attitude of rejoicing?

*You will winnow them, the wind will
pick them up, and a gale will blow them
away. But you will rejoice in the LORD
and glory in the Holy One of Israel.*

ISAIAH 41:16

Rejoicing in the Lord demonstrates our willingness to trust God so much that our attitudes are affected. When we make up our minds to rely on Him in storm and sunshine, our burdens are lifted even if our circumstances, for the moment, are unchanged or deteriorating. When we stand on His promises, our spirits are elevated and our emotions lift upward as our perspective shifts Godward. Perhaps your spirits are low right now; mine often are. But it is unhelpful and even unholy to remain in such a condition.

John Wesley, the founder of Methodism, was blessed with a spry and resilient spirit. When a collection of his letters was published, his friend, Samuel Bradburn, wrote an introduction to the volume and used the occasion to describe Wesley's uncanny ability to remain buoyant of spirit:

> I never saw him low-spirited in my life, nor could he endure to be with a melancholy person. When speaking of any who

imagined religion would make people morose or gloomy, I have heard him say in the pulpit, that "sour godliness is the devil's religion." In his answer to a letter I had written to him (in a time of strong temptation), he has these words: "(Your) melancholy turn is directly opposite to a Christian spirit. Every believer ought to enjoy life." He never suffered himself to be carried away by extreme grief. I heard him say, "I dare no more fret than curse and swear."[1]

Wesley's natural enthusiasm was buttressed by a firm belief that worry was as wrong as cursing and swearing. He understood Philippians 4:4. Rejoicing isn't just a good idea, a pleasant suggestion, or a laudable quality. God's people are to enjoy life. God wants you to enjoy life, even today. It is a command from the God of all joy who doesn't want His children doubting His providence, distrusting His promises, or discounting His sovereignty.

Think about a recent event or experience that caused you to be less than joyful. Think about your actions and how that created worry and anxiety for you. How would God have wanted you to handle that situation?

*But I trust in your unfailing love. I will
rejoice because you have rescued me.*

PSALM 13:5 NLT

Rejoicing in the Lord is not only a command we obey; it's a choice we make. God doesn't give us commandments without providing the grace needed to fulfill them. I've learned the hard way that I must exercise control over my own attitudes. More accurately, I must let the Holy Spirit have control over them. I don't have to live at the mercy of my feelings. I can choose to smile, to get up off the ground, to cast a heavenward glance, and to decide I'm going to serve the LORD with gladness. Frankly, it's hard to do. I couldn't do it without the truth of Scripture and the grace of God. There comes a time when we say, "I'm tired of living in fear when God has told me to walk by faith and to rejoice in Him always. I'm going to change my *outlook* to an *uplook*, even if I have to force myself to adopt a better attitude."

We all battle discouragement. We struggle with anxiety. But with the power of Scripture and the indwelling of the Holy Spirit, we can learn to regulate our emotions. Perhaps we can't avoid being downcast, but we don't have to remain in that condition. We can say with the writer of Psalm 42, "Why, my soul, are you downcast? Why so disturbed within me? Put your hope in God"

(v. 5). We can't afford the luxury of staying depressed or angry or anxious or fearful. We must acclimatize our minds to a higher plane by learning to rejoice in the LORD.

Ask yourself, "Why, my soul, are you downcast? Why so disturbed within me?"

What is one concrete way you can change your outlook and regulate your emotions today?

Yet I will rejoice in the LORD, I will be joyful in God my Savior.

HABAKKUK 3:18

In the Bible, every syllable is important, even the prepositions. Take the phrase *rejoice in the LORD*. We can't always rejoice in our circumstances. We certainly can't delight in the people or problems that are plaguing us. We can't always rejoice in the state of the world or the status of our homes, marriages, jobs, health, or balance sheets. Those things are a poor basis for joy. But whatever the circumstances, we can always rejoice in our LORD.

That means we rejoice in His presence, for in His presence is fullness of joy.

We rejoice in His precepts and promises, for there is a God-given promise in the Bible to counteract every anxious thought or stressful spot in life. Psalm 19:8 says, "The precepts of the LORD are right, giving joy to the heart."

We can rejoice in His providence, for we know that all things work together for good to those who love Him (Romans 8:28).

We can rejoice in His pardon, for with His forgiveness comes restoration of His joy. We can rejoice in His paths and purposes for our lives. We can rejoice in His provision, for our God will supply all our needs (Philippians 4:19).

We can rejoice in His protection, for He will never leave us nor forsake us. We can rejoice in His paradise, for to live is Christ and to die is gain (Philippians 1:21).

In any and every situation, even when we can find few other reasons for happiness, we can rejoice in our LORD and in His attributes and in His infinite fellowship and grace. The best way to generate joy in your life is to cultivate a relationship with Jesus and let Him transform your personality by renewing your thoughts (Romans 12:1–2; 1 Thessalonians 5:16–18).

How can you rejoice in His presence today?

How can you strengthen your relationship with Jesus so He can transform and renew your thoughts?

Therefore I will praise you,
LORD, among the nations;
I will sing the praises of your name.

2 SAMUEL 22:50

When I was a student at Columbia International University, the faculty and upperclassmen often told stories about one of CIU's graduates, Joy Ridderhof, the head of a missions organization known as Gospel Recordings, Inc. Joy wasn't necessarily joyful by temperament; she was a worrier. But her attitude began to change when she heard a sermon by Dr. Robert C. McQuilkin, who called worry a sin. He said it was "an offense against God as heinous as any crime man can commit."

Joy chose to replace her penchant for worry with a routine of rejoicing. She decided on an experiment. Joy sought to deliberately trust God and praise Him for His willingness and ability to bring good out of everything—including her own mistakes. She adopted James 1:2 as her key verse: "Consider it pure joy, my brothers and sisters, whenever you face trials of many kinds."

By a diligent study and application of Bible verses about rejoicing, Joy began to live up to her name and to change the very fabric of her personality. Throughout her life she dealt with loneliness, financial insecurity, ill health, difficult climates, exotic cultures, travel fatigue, and foreign governments, but she stubbornly met each difficulty with a determination to rejoice in the LORD.

In my library, I have a small booklet by Joy Ridderhof that tells of a period of time when, quite suddenly and out of a blue sky, as it were, she relapsed into worry and was overwhelmed with a burden of depression that seemed unbearable. "But from the start," she said, "I set my soul to praise the Lord even more than usual. I sang and rejoiced and the worse it became, the more I expressed praise and worship and thanksgiving to Christ. . . . I . . . knew God, through rejoicing, would be released to do mighty things in my life."[2]

I don't recall ever meeting Joy Ridderhof. I don't think I ever heard her speak in person. But even hearing others speak about her and her commitment to rejoice had an effect on me as a student.

Has someone inspired you to embrace a more joyous outlook?

How has a routine of rejoicing helped you calm your anxiety?

He will once again fill your mouth with
laughter and your lips with shouts of joy.

JOB 8:21 NLT

J oy is a climate we create around us that provides fresh air for those who share our environment.

We have to work on acclimatizing ourselves in this way. For example, I've found it helpful to avoid artificial sadness. I no longer watch sad movies or listen to melancholy music. There is enough sadness in life without generating more of it with my choices in entertainment. There are times to weep, to mourn, and to grapple with heartbreak. But God does not want us to remain bogged down in such a state, nor does He want us to foster misery like the paid mourners at ancient funerals. The underlying attitude that serves as the bedrock of our emotions should be the joy of the LORD. We must learn to process our emotions in a way that allows us to continually cycle back to joy.

I'd rather be upbeat than beat up, and I don't want others to be beat up or cast down by my attitude. Our attitudes are as contagious as the flu, and it's important to do for others what Paul was doing for the Philippians. Remember—your attitude is the climate control setting for your marriage, home, school, or workplace.

Is there something you can avoid so you can create a more positive and inviting environment?

Can you think of a time where your negative attitude was contagious like the flu? How about a time where your positive attitude was contagious? How did each attitude affect those around you?

But let the godly rejoice. Let them be glad in God's presence. Let them be filled with joy.

PSALM 68:3 NLT

Katie Hoffman wrote an encouraging book entitled *A Life of Joy*, in which she described her efforts to teach herself to rejoice in the LORD even when things are far from perfect in her circumstances or home:

> From my own experience I know that it's hard to rejoice always, especially when my husband may not be doing what I want him to do. Though I feel like wanting to show him I'm upset by acting downcast, the Holy Spirit still reminds me to rejoice always. I've had to learn, sometimes on my face, that I need to rejoice always no matter what's happening to me or around me. I have had to learn that I can't ever let the actions of other people cause me to sin. I need to be holy before the LORD despite what any other person in all the world does. This is why I emphasize so often how necessary it is for us to keep our minds fixed on things above.
>
> And regardless of how angry or upset I may want to

get at a situation, I still have to be filled with love, joy, peace, patience, kindness, goodness, gentleness, faith, and self-control (Galatians 5:22–23). I've also learned from experience that this can be almost impossible if I'm not set on glorifying the Lord Jesus at any and every cost.[3]

When we establish that climate, the sun of righteousness rises with healing in His rays, and every morning brings fresh assurance of God's great faithfulness, mercy, and love (Malachi 4:2). That bolsters our spirits and spans an enthusiastic life.

Have you allowed the actions of other people to influence your anxiety?

What Scripture verse can you memorize to help you rejoice in the Lord when you're feeling the actions of others?

*Whatever you do, do it enthusiastically,
as something done for the Lord and not
for men, knowing that you will receive
the reward of an inheritance from the
Lord. You serve the Lord Christ.*

COLOSSIANS 3:23–24 HCSB

A few years ago, I read Harry Bollback's memoir and had the opportunity to meet him and his wife, Millie, after speaking at a conference at Word of Life Bible Institute in New York.

I asked him the one question that had perplexed me from his book. Near the end of his memoirs, Harry had written, "The one thing I do wish I could do all over again for the Lord, though, would be to have a little more enthusiasm than I had."[4]

"Harry," I said, "I've seldom read a story of so much energy, passion, adventure, and excitement as yours. Why did you wish you had lived with more enthusiasm?"

"Oh, Jack Wyrtzen!" he replied, speaking of his coworker. "He was the one with enthusiasm! I wish I'd had enthusiasm like Jack's. He could get anything done because of his enthusiasm. He was the most enthusiastic man I've ever known. He showed me that if you have enthusiasm, you can do anything, you can get anything done. I wish I had done everything with a little more enthusiasm!"

I'm with Harry. Looking back on my life, I wish I had done everything with more enthusiasm. Enthusiasm is simply joy translated into daily life. When we rejoice in the LORD always, we're living with enthusiasm, and enthusiasm makes the difference.

You and I can begin today! Start immediately by memorizing Philippians 4:4 and inscribing it on the walls of your mind. It's easy to learn: "Rejoice in the Lord always. I will say it again: Rejoice!" Repeat it often. Turn it into a song. Adopt it as a slogan. Practice this verse in all its dimensions. Practice it wholeheartedly.

Repeat, "Rejoice in the LORD always." Ask yourself, "What does rejoicing in the LORD mean today?"

Let your gentleness be evident to all.

PHILIPPIANS 4:5

Richard and Arlene Baughman were married in 1940, just before America entered World War II. Richard was drafted in 1942 and left for the war just a few weeks after the birth of their first son. For more than a year, he was unable to communicate much with his family, and when he returned to his Wisconsin home he bore the scars of posttraumatic stress from combat experiences. He had a lot of bad dreams. But he and Arlene picked up where they left off, and in the years since they have faced everything together. Richard worked as a mail carrier and farmer. Arlene was a schoolteacher. They lived a busy life and raised six children, one of whom passed away. Over the years the Baughmans have encountered all the stresses and strains that come with life, just like you and me.

But here's what sets them apart. Recently this couple celebrated their seventy-fifth anniversary. Richard is now ninety-seven and Arlene is ninety-six years old. Somehow their story got out, and they've been in the news—especially because of an almost unbelievable part of their testimony. In seventy-five years of marriage, they said, they had never had a single argument. Not one. "If we had differences we just talked about it," they said. "We didn't have dishes to throw or shoes to throw because we couldn't afford it. So, we had to get along!"[5]

They explained that whenever they felt angry they would give themselves time to cool off before talking it through, and they've always taken time for regular dates and for occasional trips and vacations. They've worked hard, lived simply, not coveted too much, and have tried not to complain to each other. "The couple's advice for a happy marriage," said a reporter who interviewed them, "is to not fret over the small things and to keep faith in the Lord alive."[6]

What small things are weighing you down? What can you commit to letting go today?

Let your conversation be always full of grace, seasoned with salt, so that you may know how to answer everyone.

COLOSSIANS 4:6

I looked up all twenty-three occurrences of the word *gentle* in the Bible, and based on those references I want to suggest my own definition. When Scripture talks about gentleness it refers to "the ability to stay calm in all our conflicts and kind in all our conduct."

It doesn't mean weakness. It means that in any given situation we've developed the inner resources to remain as calm and kind as is possible under the circumstances. That's one of the greatest assets we can possess. It's a supernatural quality and a spiritual temper of soul. It is Jesus living through us, because we're not like that on our own. This is a biblical quality, and it's vital to developing a Christian personality.

Think of your interactions with your children, your spouse, your coworkers, the clerks behind the counters of coffee shops and discount stores, and even the nuisance callers on the phone. Are you consistently pleasant, calm, and kind?

Yes, there are times to be abrupt and adamant. There are moments to draw a line, to stand up for ourselves, to argue a point, to establish boundaries, and to remain true to what's right. Yet we should always do so as gently as possible in any given circumstance. There is never a moment when we should be one degree harsher than we must. We should always be as gentle as possible, and our gentleness should manifest itself in our eyes, in our facial expressions, in our body posture, in the tone of our voices, and in our subsequent actions.

How can you be more gentle today? How can you build off that gentleness and allow it to become a fabric of your existence?

You should clothe yourselves instead with the beauty that comes from within, the unfading beauty of a gentle and quiet spirit, which is so precious to God.

1 PETER 3:4 NLT

Recently while reading in the biblical book of Numbers during my morning devotions, I was struck by the critical attitudes of the children of Israel in the desert. Their constant complaining resembled smokestacks billowing out smog at full blast, and I grew convicted about my own tendency to grumble and whine about my workload, my fatigue, my busyness, my aches and pains, and all the rest of it.

In his book *Breakfast with Fred*, management consultant Fred Smith told of his friend Ron Glosser, who was the head of the Hershey Trust Company in Hershey, Pennsylvania. Glosser said that when he found himself being overly critical, the problem was likely to be in his own heart rather than in the other person's behavior. He said, "I have found that the best way to keep from being overly critical is to get myself centered early in the day. For me, this is achieved by reading the Scriptures and praying. I try to identify myself as the beloved child of God and to see all those with whom I come in contact that same way."[7]

When we fail to do this, we face needless tension. Some people keep everyone torn up. They are always involved in conflict and raise stress levels wherever they go. Difficult or demanding people put a lot of pressure on themselves and others.

Some people create anxiety for themselves and for others by disagreeableness, by their sharp tongues, by their opinionated personalities, and by their irritable spirits. When you're upset, you upset others, which piles on layers of stress like wet blankets. If you're angry at home, you'll upset your marriage. If you're harsh at work, you'll have more conflicts.

To reduce anxiety, then, develop a gentle spirit.

Can you think of a time recently when you were overly critical and harsh? How could you have dealt with the situation with more gentleness?

Take my yoke upon you. Let me teach you,
because I am humble and gentle at heart,
and you will find rest for your souls.

MATTHEW 11:29 NLT

I have a small ornamental pond along the front corner of my house, and I purchased two small fish—koi. I paid six or seven dollars each for them, and they've grown very quickly. But they're so skittish we have trouble seeing them. From a distance we'll see them swimming around in their little world, but as soon as we approach, they panic. They dart back and forth as if we were going to kill and eat them, desperately looking for a rock or lily pad to hide behind. I've read articles about how to tame koi, but so far we've not established fellowship.

That resembles how we sometimes feel toward God. He rises up, towers over us, and gazes down into our little pond, and we're afraid of Him. He is vast, unbounded, absolute in all His attributes and holy in all His ways. In one respect, the proper fear of the LORD represents a healthy attitude of reverence and awe. But our LORD is also a loving God, and He did the unimaginable by jumping into the pond with us, as it were. When we see Jesus, we see the gentleness and the tenderness and the compassion of God, and according to Hosea 11:4, the LORD draws us to Himself with "gentle cords, with bands of love" (NKJV).

What have you tried to tame in your own life? Was the resistance frustrating?

Do you have a healthy fear of the LORD, or do you struggle with being afraid of Him?

*Since God chose you to be the holy people
he loves, you must clothe yourselves
with tenderhearted mercy, kindness,
humility, gentleness, and patience.*

COLOSSIANS 3:12 NLT

Sometimes when I feel particularly sinful or unworthy, I think of the verse that is spoken about Christ in both the Old and the New Testaments: "A bruised reed he will not break, and a smoldering wick he will not snuff out" (Isaiah 42:3; Matthew 12:20).

God loves you and me greatly and gently, and through Jesus Christ, He reaches out to us with all the tenderness of His nail-scarred hands. When we respond to His love and receive Him as LORD and Savior, He moves into our hearts and begins to remodel our temperaments. He permeates our personalities with nine different attitudes, which reflect His own character. These are called the "fruit of the Spirit," and one of them is gentleness. Galatians 5:19–23 says, "The acts of the flesh are obvious . . . hatred, discord, jealously, fits of rage, selfish ambition, dissensions, factions. . . . But the fruit of the Spirit is love, joy, peace, forbearance, kindness, goodness, faithfulness, gentleness, and self-control."

Notice quality number eight: gentleness.

Another passage along the same lines, Ephesians 4:1–2 says, "live a life worthy of the calling you have received. Be completely humble and gentle." In other words, when we are completely humble and completely gentle, we demonstrate a life worthy of the calling we have received.

How can being more gentle help your anxiety? How can a gentleness keep you reassured and calm?

*Together as one body, Christ reconciled
both groups to God by means of his
death on the cross, and our hostility
toward each other was put to death.*

EPHESIANS 2:16 NLT

In her book *I Never Walk the Halls Alone*, Donna Kincheloe wrote about her experiences as a critical care nurse. One of her most touching memories involved her grandfather, who had raised her. When she received word of his heart attack, she raced to his side in a Pennsylvania hospital, where she found him unable to speak. He tried desperately to communicate, but he couldn't vocalize his words. Through long experience in intensive care units, Donna had learned to read lips and she quickly realized her grandfather was pleading to see his two children, Dee and Bud. Years before, these two siblings had argued and grown embittered toward each other. They had not spoken for a dozen years. Now they met at their dying father's bedside.

"My mom and Uncle Bud wanted me there to interpret, so, next visiting time, the three of us went to Grandpa's bedside," Donna recalled. "Mom was on his left and Uncle Bud was on his right. Grandpa reached up and took Mom's right hand and Bud's left hand and put them together. He then covered their hands with his own strong mechanic's hands and mouthed two words over and over, 'Make up. Make up. Make up.'"[8]

Donna went on to suggest that Jesus, by His death, had a similar objective. He wants to reunite us with our heavenly Father and with each other, and His wounded hands can bring healing to our relationships and replace hostility with gentleness and understanding.[9]

Can you think of a time when healing a relationship brought gentleness and understanding to your life? What did you learn from the reconciliation?

May the words of my mouth and the
meditation of my heart be pleasing to you,
O LORD, my rock and my redeemer.

PSALM 19:14 NLT

According to Proverbs 25:15, a gentle tongue is stronger than a rigid bone. We could paraphrase this verse to say that a person who knows how to speak gently will be more effective in any situation than someone who is rigid and severe.

I learned this lesson when I was in high school and working at Jim Chambers Men's Shop in my hometown of Elizabethton, Tennessee. Jim was a wonderful man, a Christian, and he'd been a retailer for many years with a loyal base of customers in our community. One day while I was working in the back of the store, a man—a farmer and a hillbilly—burst into the store like a thunderclap. He was upset over a pair of shoes he had purchased. He let Jim have it, telling him how sorry the shoes were, how they hurt his feet, how they didn't fit right, how they weren't made well, how he'd been cheated. There in front of Jim and the other customers, he flew into a fit. My heart stopped and I felt a panic attack coming on. Jim just stood there, looking at the man and at the shoes and nodding thoughtfully during the rant.

When the man finished, I waited for my boss to let him have

it back. But Jim just said, "Mr. Farmer, I'm sorry you don't like your shoes. Sometimes we just get a bad pair, don't we? What would you like me to do about it? Would you like your money back? Would you like another pair of shoes? I'll be glad to give you another pair. You just pick them out. Here, I'll throw in a pair of socks."

The farmer just wilted. He looked down, his anger spent, and he said, "Well, I guess another pair of shoes would be all right, Jim."

Jim looked at me and said, "Robert, help this man find another pair of shoes." I guess Jim didn't know I panicked in confrontation, and my hands were shaking a bit as I pulled boxes off the shelves. But I got the farmer shod, and as soon as he was out the door, Jim smiled at me and said, "I lost a pair of shoes but I kept a customer."

Have you experienced a similar situation that tested your patience? How did your calm attitude impact the situation for everyone involved?

Always be prepared to give an answer to everyone who asks you to give the reason for the hope that you have. But do this with gentleness and respect.

1 PETER 3:15

Successful people cultivate the quality of gentleness, which means reining in the rougher elements of their tempers and practicing self-control with their tongues. They have learned to be calm in all their conflict and kind in all their conduct.

With a little thought, we can devise personal techniques that allow our gentleness to show through. One man did it by holding a pipe in his hand. Harold Wilson served two stints as Britain's prime minister in the 1960s and '70s. He was frequently seen with a pipe in his hand, though he preferred cigars. He ended up with that pipe in his hand because he had a bad habit of raising his hand as a fist when making a point. His adviser, Marcia Williams, felt this looked threatening to viewers, so she gave him a pipe to hold as a prop. It worked, and Wilson exuded a gentler and more confident appearance, leading to his political success.[10]

My friend Rocky Forshey of Houston, Texas, told me that years ago when his children were young he would grow upset at them and tramp through the house to scold them. Passing a mirror once, he was shocked at the fierce countenance on his face. He realized that's how his children saw him. He instantly softened his face, and he took the lesson to heart. He began practicing relaxing his expression whenever he spoke with his children, and it became a lifelong habit that has given Rocky a countenance that isn't rocky at all but gentle and wise.[11]

Do you have personal techniques that allow your gentleness to show through? If not, should you adopt one?

Always be humble and gentle. Be patient with each other, making allowance for each other's faults because of your love.

EPHESIANS 4:2 NLT

John Wooden, one of the most revered coaches in the history of college basketball, credited much of his success to his dad. He recalled a boyhood occasion when he watched his father deal with a certain situation. His rural Indiana county would pay local farmers to take teams of mules or horses into the gravel pits scattered through the county and haul out loads of gravel.

One steamy summer day, wrote Wooden, a young farmer was trying to get his team of horses to pull a fully loaded wagon out of the pit. He was whipping and cursing those beautiful plow horses, which were frothing at the mouth, stomping, and pulling back from him. The elder Wooden watched for a while, then went over to the young man and said, "Let me take 'em for you."

> Dad started talking to the horses, almost whispering to them, and stroking their noses with a soft touch. Then he walked between them, holding their bridles and bits while he continued talking—very calmly and gently—as they settled down. Gradually he stepped out in front of

them and gave a little whistle to start them moving forward while he guided the reins. Within moments, those two big plow horses pulled the wagon out of the gravel pit as easy as could be. As if they were happy to do it.[12]

John Wooden said, "I've never forgotten what I saw him do and how he did it. Over the years I've seen a lot of leaders act like that angry young farmer who lost control. . . . So much more can usually be accomplished by Dad's calm, confident, and steady approach."[13]

Wooden took away an indelible lesson: "It takes strength inside to be gentle on the outside."[14]

What can you do to be more gentle on the outside? Is there a specific area in your life that would greatly benefit from more gentleness?

*Which do you choose? Should I come
with a rod to punish you, or should I
come with love and a gentle spirit?*

1 CORINTHIANS 4:21 NLT

E cclesiastes 8:1 says, "A person's wisdom brightens their face and changes its hard appearance."

A gentle spirit reduces anxiety, reflects Christ, gets things done, and, most importantly, pleases the LORD. He is delighted when we are gentle, and He is grieved when we aren't. There's a wonderful verse about this in the Bible. It was originally addressed to women, but its message is transferable to all of us.

> Your beauty should not come from outward adornment, such as elaborate hairstyles and the wearing of gold jewelry or fine clothes. Rather, it should be that of your inner self, the unfading beauty of a gentle and quiet spirit, which is of great worth in God's sight. (1 Peter 3:3–4)

Look at those words: "a gentle . . . spirit, which is of great worth in God's sight." According to the apostle Peter, this is true elegance; and it's the way we make ourselves appealing to others, to the world, and to the LORD. When I was a boy, my parents, both schoolteachers, sometimes took me to Knoxville, Tennessee, for their educational conferences, and we always stayed downtown at the Farragut Hotel, next door to the S&W Cafeteria. One year my elderly grandparents accompanied us, and during supper my grandfather, Clifton Palmer, grew agitated. Turning to my mom, he said, "An old man across the room keeps scowling at me." We all looked, of course. The opposite wall was lined with mirrors, and my grandfather had been looking at no one but himself.

If only we could see the expression on our faces the way others see us!

If you want a more attractive face, learn to be gentle, quiet, and confident in your demeanor. Gentleness is the world's most exclusive beauty secret. If only we could bottle it! It relaxes our faces and releases our smiles. It pleases God.

How could you benefit from more quietness in your life?

Is there a Scripture about quietness that will help you build your gentleness and confidence?

*Gentle words are a tree of life; a
deceitful tongue crushes the spirit.*

PROVERBS 15:4 NLT

There's scant gentleness in our world. Just turn on the radio or television. Watch a movie. Read blog comments or social media posts. People are indignant. People are shouting at each other. People insult one another in our increasingly coarse culture. This demanding spirit can seep into our homes and churches. I confess I'm not as gentle as I should be in reacting to provocation or fatigue or stress. But as Christians we should be keen to improve. When we trust Jesus Christ as our Lord and Savior, we begin to change and we keep improving as long as we're on earth. And a gentle spirit reduces our stress, reflects Christ, gets things done, and pleases the Lord.

Remember what Saint Francis de Sales said: "Nothing is so strong as gentleness, nothing so gentle as real strength."[15] A good place to start is by memorizing and practicing Philippians 4:5: "*Let your gentleness be evident to all.*"

Have you recently encountered a challenging situation that you could have handled with more gentleness? Was it a reaction to something you heard or read? Was it an in-person reaction to someone? Think through the ways you could handle a similar situation with more gentleness.

You will fill me with joy in your presence,
with eternal pleasures at your right hand.

PSALM 16:11

During my college days, a few buddies and I were hiking somewhere in a beautiful gorge when we detoured over a ravine by walking across a fallen tree. I was halfway across the thing when I froze and got tottery. The ground seemed as if it was a mile below me. I recall flailing my arms like a windmill and shouting, "I've lost my nerve!" The friend in front of me instantly reached out and took hold of my hand. I could have pulled us both off the log, but somehow the momentary touch of my friend's hand gave stability. I regained my balance and made it safely to the other side.

I've thought of that many times when I've gotten weak-kneed over other chasms, and it's the touch of a Friend's hand that has steadied me—the bracing hand of the LORD. The same is true for the heroes of Scripture. When Peter sank in alarm trying to walk across the choppy waters of Galilee, Jesus immediately reached out His hand and caught him, saying, "You of little faith . . . why did you doubt?" (Matthew 14:31).

Think of a time when a friend or family member came to your rescue. How did they ease your worries?

Think of a time when you felt the hand of the Lᴏʀᴅ steady you. How did He ease your worries?

Remember me, Lord, when you show favor
to your people; come near and rescue me.

PSALM 106:4 NLT

When you spot a couple walking down the street hand in hand, you know they're in love. The same is true for us in our love for Jesus. We enjoy the Lord's fellowship when holding His unchanging hand, and as we cultivate a sense of His nearness, we grow increasingly intimate with Him. We're strengthened and steadied by the nearness of His touch.

The stresses of life rattle our minds. We feel uncertain and insecure. This even happened to Paul in Troas when he couldn't complete his mission (2 Corinthians 2:12–13). But the apostle worked through these issues and later penned the Bible's greatest passage against worry. His eight-point strategy in Philippians 4 begins with the practices of rejoicing and gentleness. Then it goes on to suggest we cultivate the practice of nearness. Verse 5 ends with the words: *"The Lord is near."*

I have my Bible open to Philippians 4 as I'm writing this, and it occurs to me the passage would have continued smoothly had these words been omitted. The Lord could have left them out of His Scripture and we wouldn't have known the difference: *Rejoice in the LORD always. I will say it again: Rejoice! Let your gentleness be evident to all. Do not be anxious about anything.*

But oh, how vital those four words: *The LORD is near.* How great our loss had they been left out!

Can you think of a time when the LORD's nearness eased your anxiety and helped you feel safe?

What feelings does the phrase "the LORD is near" elicit in you? Consider repeating this phrase to yourself when you feel your anxiety ratcheting up and see whether it brings calm to your spirit.

You, too, must be patient. Take courage,
for the coming of the Lord is near.

JAMES 5:8 NLT

The phrase "The LORD is near," can refer to His closeness to us. It can also refer to the nearness of His second coming. His return is near!

The Bible was written from God's perspective, and His concept of nearness is different from ours. To God, the time between our LORD's first and second comings is just a moment. From the vantage point of eternity, it's just a day or two. Peter pointed this out to critics in the first century who were impatient for the LORD's return and who demanded, "Where is this 'coming' he promised?" (2 Peter 3:4).

Peter replied, "Do not forget this one thing, dear friends: With the Lord a day is like a thousand years, and a thousand years are like a day. The Lord is not slow in keeping his promise, as some understand slowness" (vv. 8–9).

To our everlasting God, a thousand years resemble the passing of a single day. From the vantage of eternity, then, Jesus has only been gone from earth a couple of days. He understands nearness and slowness from a different frame of reference. We dwell in time, but we share Christ's everlasting life. Believers in every generation have expected Jesus to come in their lifetimes, which is how it should be. The LORD wants us to live with anticipation and readiness, and, from His perspective, we may well be down to the last hours or minutes. His coming is soon, as He understands soon-ness, and that's good enough for me.

How can you use Paul's perspective, regarding the vantage point of eternity, to help you deal with your anxious feelings?

*For our light and momentary troubles
are achieving for us an eternal glory
that far outweighs them all.*

2 CORINTHIANS 4:17

Sometimes when I'm overwhelmed with worry or with the weight of my problems, I remind myself that fifty years from now, I'll not be worried about any of this (unless I still manage to be alive at 120). When the LORD takes His children out of the world, they're released from all their problems, and this provides great solace. Jesus told the thief on the cross beside Him, "Truly I tell you, today you will be with me in paradise" (Luke 23:43).

One of the things we most look forward to about heaven is freedom from every worry, anxiety, and care. Revelation 21:4 says, "'He will wipe every tear from their eyes. There will be no more death' or mourning or crying or pain, for the old order of things has passed away."

We're presently part of the old order of things. We're living under a curse that fell across the universe because of sin. But for Christ-followers, our problems are temporary and our burdens are momentary, but our blessings are permanent. Whatever we're worrying about now will be of no concern to us a hundred years from now. God will release us from all our troubles and work them all for our good. He'll take over our problems and resolve them for His glory, and we can rest in a glorious future. A poet from the past said:

> *Not now, but in the coming years,*
> *It may be in the better land,*
> *We'll read the meaning of our tears,*
> *And there, some time, we'll understand.*[16]

What burdens or troubles are causing you anxiety that you should release?

Their mind is set on earthly things. But our citizenship is in heaven. And we eagerly await a Savior from there, the Lord Jesus Christ, who, by the power that enables him to bring everything under his control, will transform our lowly bodies so that they will be like his glorious body.

PHILIPPIANS 3:19-21

When I was a little boy, ten or eleven years old, my dad promised to take us to Myrtle Beach, South Carolina, on vacation. We'd been there before, and I can't tell you how excited I was. I loved going to Myrtle Beach, chowing down on pancakes in the morning, playing in the ocean all day, riding everything at the carnival in the evening, playing miniature golf, and having my parents' full attention for the whole week.

My little sister, Ann, was about five, and I wanted her to be as excited about the trip as I was. I wrote to the Myrtle Beach Chamber of Commerce asking for brochures. A week or so later, I began getting brochures by the dozens from every attraction, amusement park, hotel, restaurant, and golf course on the Grand Strand. I organized them on a folding table and went over every brochure with Ann. I had her so excited she could hardly sleep at night. We were so wound up with anticipation, we could almost have flown there by flapping our arms.

In the week before we left, I might have gotten into trouble with my parents. I might have worried about a lost library book. Maybe I had a flat tire on my bicycle. I probably scraped my knee. But I recovered from all such problems more quickly because I was busy packing for the beach. The anticipation of the trip eclipsed everything else in my life.

I still love going to Myrtle Beach, and I get great joy anticipating other trips as well. But there's one destination I'm looking forward to above all. In times of anxiety or distress I remind myself, "None of these problems are going to matter to me in a few years. All my worries are short-lived, and in any event God has promised they will somehow turn out for good."

Are you planning a vacation or weekend getaway? What destination are you anticipating?

Abraham lived in tents and weathered the troubles of life by faith, "for he was looking forward to the city with foundations, whose architect and builder is God . . . longing for a better country—a heavenly one."

HEBREWS 11:10, 16

Can you see how eternal anticipation is an antidote to current frustration? The regular contemplation of the LORD's return and of heaven is an essential biblical therapy for worry. The Bible is all about the future. Page after page and passage after passage is devoted to prophecy, to what's ahead, to the resurrection, to the return of Christ, to the endless adventures of everlasting life.

The next time you fall into an anxious state, take a deep breath, put your problem on hold, find a quiet spot, and read Revelation 21–22. It's the Bible's travel brochure of heaven. Picture the diamond city of New Jerusalem descending like a jewel to the new earth. Visualize the streets, walls, gates, throne, and crystal river. Read 1 Thessalonians 4 about the moment of Christ's return. Study prophecy. See what the Bible says about the future. Our burdens cannot follow us to heaven, and our trials and troubles are not worth comparing to the glory that will be revealed in us.

What are you anticipating the most about heaven? In Revelation 21–22, what stands out to you?

Is there a specific verse in Revelation 21–22 that you connect with deeply? Memorize this verse and say it to yourself when feeling frustrated by your current circumstances.

*You are near, O Lord, and all
your commands are true.*

PSALM 119:151 NLT

It's true that God is everywhere at once—omnipresent—in every location of every realm in the visible and invisible spheres. God is not measurable, and the essence of His personality fills the galaxies and extends beyond the limits of the universe, traversing all the territories of fathomless infinity. He occupies every address, inhabits every sector, tracks every vector, and resides in every corner of the universe. He fills heaven and earth.

Yet in a personal way, our LORD draws near and speaks to us in times of stress, worry, anxiety, or fear. As I look back over my adult life, I've had a lot of times when I've been overtaken with anxiety. I've had times when I almost suffocated with worry. But what I remember most about those times is how they drove me to sit down, open my Bible, cry out to the LORD, pray to Him, and find specific Bible verses that calmed me down and gave me strength and courage. Those have become my favorite verses today.

That's the privilege of every Christian, and it's not just a matter of studying a book. It's a matter of meeting with a living Person and touching an unseen hand. Even now, I'm writing these words in an empty hotel room, and I've been fighting off some nagging worries. But this isn't an empty hotel room. It's as full of the LORD's presence as the holy of holies, where the LORD Himself would reside in the Jewish temple. When I remind myself of that, reality enters the picture.

What is a Bible verse that calms you down, that provides you with strength and courage?

How has the LORD spoken to you in times of stress and anxiety?

*Give to the LORD the glory he deserves! Bring
your offering and come into his presence.
Worship the LORD in all his holy splendor.*

1 CHRONICLES 16:29 NLT

In a sense, learning to actualize God's presence is the very definition of revival. Perhaps like you, I'm longing for a new great tsunami of revival to flood our land, and in my studies of the great revivals of the past, the most significant aspect is an intense and unusual awareness of an almost supernatural sense of God's proximity.

Mrs. Hester Rendall told me of working with Rev. Duncan Campbell in the 1950s on the Hebrides Island of Lewis. There had been an intense revival there between 1949 and 1952. Though Hester didn't arrive until 1958, the afterglow of the revival was still evident. One evening she went to a church service and a sense of the presence of the LORD came down so strongly that the people prayed earnestly and hardly dared lift their heads. After a while, Hester's friend leaned over to her and suggested they go home. Hester said, "Why? We've only been here a few minutes."

The friend said, "It's three o'clock in the morning."

Those who study revivals come across story after story like

that, in which the intensity of the presence of God comes into a geographical zone so strongly that people can almost feel it, are awed by it, and are brought to instant conviction, conversion, and confidence.

Have you had a similar experience? Where were you and how did you feel when you walked away?

If not, have you read or heard about a revival experience that you found convicting and life-changing?

But as for me, how good it is to be near God! I have made the Sovereign LORD my shelter, and I will tell everyone about the wonderful things you do.

PSALM 73:28 NLT

The chief purpose of prayer is to recognize the presence of the LORD. Someone once asked evangelist Dwight L. Moody how he managed to remain so intimate in his relationship with Christ. He replied:

> I have come to Him as the best friend I have ever found, and I can trust Him in that relationship. I have believed He is Savior; I have believed He is God; I have believed His atonement on the cross is mine, and I have come to Him and submitted myself on my knees, surrendered everything to Him, and got up and stood by His side as my friend, and there isn't any problem in my life, there isn't any uncertainty in my work but I turn and speak to Him as naturally as to someone in the same room, and I have done it these years because I can trust Jesus.[17]

Whatever your burdens today, remember the practice of joy, the practice of gentleness, the practice of nearness, both in terms of His imminent coming and His immediate presence. Those are the starting points in the Bible's strategy for ridding yourself of chronic worry.

Try to learn these simple principles by heart:

"Rejoice in the Lord always. I will say it again: Rejoice!
Let your gentleness be evident to all.
The Lord is near.
Do not be anxious about anything."

What can you do to be more joyous in your day-to-day?

*Give all your worries and cares to
God, for he cares about you.*

1 PETER 5:7 NLT

The better we grasp the boundless sovereignty of God, the less we'll worry about the everyday burdens of life. If we anchor our hearts in the bottomless depths of Christ's love, nothing can capsize us. When we truly claim the inexhaustible wealth of the Spirit's deposit, we'll be rich in the peace that transcends understanding.

Eugene Peterson's Bible paraphrase, *The Message*, states Philippians 4:6–7 like this: "Don't fret or worry. Instead of worrying, pray. Let petitions and praises shape your worries into prayers, letting God know your concerns. Before you know it, a sense of God's wholeness, everything coming together for good, will come and settle you down. It's wonderful what happens when Christ displaces worry at the center of your life."

If this advice were given only here in the Bible, it would still be wonderful and welcomed, but it is *not* given only here. This particular Greek word, *merimnao*, appears several times in the Bible, and these occurrences are consistent in their teaching and represent a divine inoculation against the paralyzing disease of worry.

What are you worried about right now? Take a moment and pray. Let go of that worry and give your worries to the LORD.

What do you think of *The Message*'s translation of Philippians 4:6–7? Is there another Bible translation of this passage that you particularly like?

But each day the Lord pours his unfailing love upon me, and through each night I sing his songs, praying to God who gives me life.

PSALM 42:8 NLT

What exactly is the process by which we transfer our cares to God and tap into His peace for ourselves? There is only one way to do that—through prayer. Earnest, heartfelt, biblical prayer is the method by which we transfer our legitimate worries into the Lord's mighty hands, and by which He transfers His inexpressible peace into our fragile hearts.

Prayer is the closet where we change clothes and replace a spirit of despair with a garment of praise. It's the bank where we present the promissory notes of God's promises and withdraw endless deposits of grace. It's the darkroom of the soul where negatives become positives. It's the transfer station where the pulse of fear is exchanged for the impulse of faith. It's a currency exchange where we trade in our liabilities for God's abundant life. This is biblical replacement therapy, and it's the duty of the child of God to learn how to displace worrisome thoughts with restorative strength through prevailing prayer, and to do it in every situation.

The life of faith is a growing experience, and prayer is an ongoing process of abiding in our Father's presence, meeting with

Him at every turn, consulting Him in every plight, and trusting Him with every trial. In prayer, we transfer our problems to the LORD, and He transfers His peace to us. That allows us to rid ourselves of the false guilt we sometimes feel when we stop worrying.

Can you think of a time when prayer took away your worries, or provided grace or abundance in your life?

I pray that God, the source of hope, will fill you completely with joy and peace because you trust in him. Then you will overflow with confident hope through the power of the Holy Spirit.

ROMANS 15:13 NLT

Sometimes we don't want to stop worrying because it seems wrong to feel lighthearted. We don't want to react flippantly or inappropriately to life's heartaches. But in every situation, our supernatural LORD wants to lighten our hearts and lift the clouds of uneasiness. Things are never as bad as they seem where He is concerned. All His resources are available through prayer, and none of His promises have expired. So stop worrying and start praying, taking time to especially note those items for which you can be thankful.

Our refusal to worry doesn't mean we aren't concerned, nor does it make us passive to circumstances. Concern is appropriate, and wise responses are needed, but worry is unhelpful. The zone between concern and worry is a slippery slope. I've often wondered how to know, at any given time, if I'm reasonably concerned or unreasonably alarmed. It's a difficult median, but here's the key: When our concern is healthy in nature, it doesn't debilitate us. When it begins to feel debilitating, it has morphed into worry, which becomes a vicious cycle. I don't know about you, but sometimes I worry myself sick over how worried I am that I'm worried.

When worry barges into our brains, it brings along a gang of accomplices—discouragement, fear, exhaustion, despair, anguish, hopelessness, pain, obsession, distraction, foreboding, irritation, impatience—none of which are friends of the Holy Spirit. We have to throw the bums out of our hearts and minds. Prayer is how we open the door, shove them out, and let the peace of God rush in to secure our thoughts and feelings.

Think of three worries you can toss away. How will letting these worries go change your day, week, and month?

I will answer them before they even call to me.
While they are still talking about their needs,
I will go ahead and answer their prayers!

ISAIAH 65:24 NLT

Not long ago a New Zealand pilot named Owen B. Wilson wanted to do something special for his friend Grant Stubbs, who was celebrating a birthday. Wilson offered to take his friend flying in a two-seat, micro-light plane. The two men took off after church on Sunday from the South Island town of Blenheim in the Marlborough region, flying northeast over the Golden Bay, around hills and over gorgeous landscapes and seascapes along the northern tip of the island. But as they crossed a tall mountain, the engine sputtered and died. The plane began losing altitude, and at that point Wilson could see nothing but steep mountainsides descending into a treacherous sea.

Both men were Christians and they prayed instantly and earnestly. When it appeared the two would fly into a mountain, Stubbs cried: "Lord, please help us to get over that steep ledge!"

They skimmed over the ridge, and Grant began praying, "Lord, we need to find somewhere to land!" Just when all hope seemed gone, the men saw a small strip of land almost hidden between two ridges. Wilson steered the plane in that direction. They glided into the narrow valley and touched down, bouncing to a stop. They both shouted, "Thank You, Lord!"

They looked up and just in front of them was a huge twenty-foot sign that said, "Jesus is Lord!"

As it turned out, the field belonged to a Christian retreat center, which explained the billboard. The owners, who ran out to greet their unexpected guests, told them the field was usually full of livestock, but on this day all the animals were standing along the edge of the field, as though giving the plane room to land.[18]

Many times we fly into anxious situations in life. But in every situation we practice the power of prayer, and that's how we discover the incredible truth that Jesus is LORD.

What was an instant prayer response that you received from the LORD?

*Great is his faithfulness; his mercies
begin afresh each morning.*

LAMENTATIONS 3:23 NLT

When I was nineteen, I had mentors who impressed on me the importance of beginning my day with morning devotions, and this habit has kept me afloat for fifty-one years. After arising and showering in the morning, I sit down at a small upstairs desk where I briefly jot down a few lines in my journal, read God's Word, work on some verse or another that I'm memorizing, and open up my prayer lists, thanking God for His blessings and asking for His intervention in things concerning me. I often pray aloud. Before leaving the spot, I consult my calendar and jot out a proposed agenda for the day. Psalm 143:8 says, "Let the morning bring me word of your unfailing love, for I have put my trust in you. Show me the way I should go, for to you I entrust my life."

It's as simple as that, but nothing goes right about my day if I neglect the practice.

Perhaps the morning hour doesn't fit your schedule. It's not a matter of having a time of *morning* prayer but of *daily* prayer, whenever works best. The things that mean most to us are the things we do daily. That's the glue of life that holds everything together. Jesus told us to go into our inner rooms and shut the door and talk to our heavenly Father in secret (Matthew 6:6). This implies a definite time and place for meeting privately with God in a way that allows us to realize and recognize His presence, which, after all, is the intent of Philippians 4:5–6: "The Lord is near. . . . In every situation, by prayer and petition . . . present your requests to God."

What does your daily prayer routine look like? If you don't have a prayer routine, create one. Dedicate a time and space for your daily prayer.

Search me, O God, and know my heart;
test me and know my anxious thoughts.

PSALM 139:23 NLT

F ew of us lose sleep over cosmic threats until they're brought home to us in an immediate way. Most of our worries are closer at hand. But whether our concerns are intergalactic or interpersonal, we exist in an anxious world that skips along the edges of danger and difficulty. No one knows what the next hour or day will bring. Yet the Bible directs us to live beyond the pale of worry. We are told emphatically: "Do not worry about anything" (Philippians 4:6 NCV). We must take every word of Philippians 4:6 as holy counsel to be instantly and thoroughly obeyed: "Do not be anxious about anything, but in every situation, by prayer and petition, with thanksgiving, present your requests to God."

In a world where we're frustrated by everything from the fragility of complex systems to the complexity of our entertainment systems, we need to nurture thankful hearts and minds full of gratitude.

Try this experiment. Read Philippians 4:6 (NKJV) aloud, leaving out the words "with thanksgiving." Say the verse like this:

> Be anxious for nothing,
> but in everything by prayer and supplication,
> let your requests be made known to God.

Now try it God's way and emphasize the phrase "with thanksgiving."

> Be anxious for nothing,
> but in everything by prayer and supplication,
> *with thanksgiving,*
> let your requests be made known to God.

The verse sounds reasonable either way, but the addition of "with thanksgiving" adds a dimension that melts away anxiety like winter's ice on a sunny day. No matter our crisis or concern, there are always notable items for which we can be thankful, and finding them is critical to calming your anxiety.

Science has proven that gratitude helps people feel more positive emotions, improves their health, helps when dealing with adversity, and builds strong relationships. Think of (or write down) three things you are grateful for. Incorporate this gratitude process into your daily routine.

*Be thankful in all circumstances, for this is
God's will for you who belong to Christ Jesus.*

1 THESSALONIANS 5:18 NLT

In his book *Thanks! How Practicing Gratitude Can Make You Happier*, Dr. Robert A. Emmons of the University of California, Davis, explains how each of us is born with certain preset elements to our personalities. Just as each of us has a unique and individual body, so each of us has a unique and individual personality. According to Dr. Emmons, "Current psychological dogma states that one's capacity for joy is biologically set."[19]

He wrote: "Each person appears to have a set-point for happiness. . . . Each person has a chronic or characteristic level of happiness. According to this idea, people have happiness set-points to which they inevitably return following disruptive life events."[20]

But Dr. Emmons has done innovative research to demonstrate there is one quality that, if developed and practiced, can actually change our set-point for happiness. We can change the gauges of our personalities in an upward and happier direction if we deliberately work on improving our habits of gratitude and thanksgiving.

Emmons wrote:

We discovered scientific proof that when people regularly engage in a systematic cultivation of gratitude, they experience a variety of measurable benefits: psychological, physical, and interpersonal. The evidence on gratitude contradicts the widely held view that all people have a "setpoint" of happiness that cannot be reset by any known means: in some cases, people have reported that gratitude led to transformative life changes.[21]

He concluded, "Our groundbreaking research has shown that grateful people experience higher levels of positive emotions such as joy, enthusiasm, love, happiness and optimism, and that the practice of gratitude as a discipline protects a person from the destructive impulses of envy, resentment, greed, and bitterness."[22]

What are you currently doing to cultivate more gratitude in your life? How can you increase or cultivate even more gratitude?

"What do you mean, 'If I can'?" Jesus asked.
"Anything is possible if a person believes."
MARK 9:23 NLT

Worry pulls your mind apart, like a man being drawn and quartered. It rips and ruptures your thoughts and feelings. It makes you feel as though you're being torn in two.

What should do that to us? Nothing! Absolutely nothing!

The older translations of Philippians 4:6 say emphatically: "In nothing be anxious." In a book of remarkable statements, this one is near the top. *Nothing* should agitate us, because *nothing* can separate us from the love of a God for whom *nothing* is impossible.

Each day share your concerns with God through prayer. Instead of allowing your anxiety to take over your existence, share your worries with Christ, and give Him the opportunity to displace your worry. Oftentimes, we get caught in the busyness of our day-to-day and we trick ourselves into thinking that we can manage everything. When we're feeling exhausted, overwhelmed, or frightened we think we have the ability to overcome. However, it's only with God by our sides that we're able to not be anxious and allow the impossible to be possible.

What impossible circumstance did God make possible for you? How did that change your perspective on His love for you?

Do you believe that nothing can separate you from the love of God? Do you take your worries to Him so He has the opportunity to remove them?

Then Jesus said, "Come to me, all of you who are weary and carry heavy burdens, and I will give you rest."

MATTHEW 11:28 NLT

Anxiety is so deeply ingrained into my personality that I feel guilty when I *don't* worry. When something is deeply troubling me, I feel responsible to worry about it. There's a moral obligation, so it seems, to worry about those things that should logically worry me. How can I shrug off issues that so deeply affect those I love and me? If I don't worry, who will?

Well, that's the point.

As we turn our worries over to the LORD, He goes to work on them. He is able to guard what we have entrusted to Him (2 Timothy 1:12). God, being God, doesn't worry, but He does work. The psalmist said, "It is time for you to act, LORD" (Psalm 119:126). And God can do far more by His action than we can do by our anxiety. According to Ephesians 1:11, God has plans and purposes that work out everything in conformity with the purpose of His will. According to Romans 8:28, all things work out for our good. Sometimes we find ourselves shipwrecked on Omnipotence and stranded on Sovereignty.[23]

We're much better off when Jehovah-Shalom, the LORD of peace, bears the lion's share of our burdens. But what exactly is the process by which we transfer our cares to God and tap into His peace for ourselves? Prayer. Coming to the LORD, earnestly asking Him for guidance and peace, is the only way to transfer our valid concerns not His capable hands. In return, the LORD transfers his peace into our worried hearts.

Do you find yourself feeling guilty for not worrying? What Scripture verse can you memorize and turn to when you're overwhelmed with worry?

You faithfully answer our prayers with
awesome deeds, O God our savior.
You are the hope of everyone on earth,
even those who sail on distant seas.

PSALM 65:5 NLT

The life of faith is a growing experience, and prayer is an ongoing process of abiding in our Father's presence, meeting with Him at every turn, consulting Him in every plight, and trusting Him with every trial. In prayer, we transfer our problems to the LORD, and He transfers His peace to us. That allows us to rid ourselves of the false guilt we sometimes feel when we stop worrying.

If we live long enough, perhaps we'll reach a level of maturity beyond all worrisome fear. I haven't reached that stage yet, and neither had the Philippians. The LORD was telling us in Philippians 4, in effect: "When you find yourself ripped apart by worry, learn to use the power of My presence through prayer to unleash divine processes that can conquer worry, demolish strongholds, effect change, and inject powerful doses of transcendent peace into your hearts, in every single situation in life."

When we are experiencing false guilt because we have conquered a worry, take this guilt to the LORD in prayer too. Allow the LORD to do what He promised in Philippians 4. When we have a solid relationship with the LORD through prayer, things are never as bad as they appear. A good way to remind ourselves of this is by including in our prayers our gratitude for people, things, and events in our lives. Remember, too Jesus' promise to us: "Peace I leave with you; my peace I give you.... Do not let your hearts be troubled and do not be afraid" (John 14:27). The LORD's promises never expire.

Can you think of something in your own life that is on the slippery slope of worry? Commit to having a conversation with the LORD and identify through prayer how to stop worrying.

Then he said, "Don't be afraid, Daniel.
Since the first day you began to pray for
understanding and to humble yourself before
your God, your request has been heard in
heaven. I have come in answer to your prayer."
DANIEL 10:12 NLT

When I'm in the midst of an anxious episode, I often find myself at a desk with my journal and an open Bible, asking God to stabilize not just the situation but me as well. I write out my fears and emotions, because stating them makes them more manageable. Then I search the Scripture to find verses that comfort my heart, and I write those down too. Then I pray aloud, sometimes writing out my prayers, sometimes pacing the room, kneeling, falling on my face, or going for a prayer walk, as I plead for God's help. Other times I'll seek out someone to pray with—such as my prayer partner or a close friend.

Sometimes our prayers are extended. Daniel and Nehemiah fasted and prayed for many weeks over certain matters. On the other hand, the tax collector in Luke 18:13 simply beat his fist against his chest and said seven words, "God, have mercy on me, a sinner."

Occasionally I'll find a phrase from Scripture to think

about repetitively whenever fear or panic rises. A good example is Matthew 6:10, which says, "Your will be done, on earth as it is in heaven." That's an all-purpose plea from the lips of Jesus that helps me know what to pray when other words fail: "LORD, Your will be done in this situation, as it's done in heaven." Whenever the tide of worry rises in my heart, I pause and deliberately pray, "LORD, may Your will be done right now in this thing." We can sense the poignancy of this phrase because at the end of His earthly life, our LORD circled back to it, saying, in the garden of Gethsemane, "May your will be done" (Matthew 26:42).

Finding phrases in the Bible is a powerful method of prayer. What phrases in the Bible can you learn to lean on?

May you have the power to understand, as all God's people should, how wide, how long, how high, and how deep his love is. May you experience the love of Christ, though it is too great to understand fully. Then you will be made complete with all the fullness of life and power that comes from God.

EPHESIANS 3:18–19 NLT

God never feels a worried moment. He dwells above all the cares of the world, inhabiting eternity and occupying infinity. He knows the end from the beginning. No threat can disturb Him and no foe can threaten Him; for He—He alone—is the Creator, Sustainer, and Commander of the universe and all it contains. He is the Ruler of all reality, in all realms, in all epochs and ages, whether seen or unseen, whether visible or invisible. His infinite power merges with limitless love to reassure His people of His obstinate providence. He can replace your transient worries with transcendent peace.

Because God is infinite, His measureless peace is never exhausted, nor even diminished, regardless of its outflow. Because He is unchanging, His peace is unwavering. Because He is almighty, His peace is all-powerful, fully able to pull down the strongholds of anxiety in our lives. Because He is omnipresent, His peace is available to every one of us, everywhere, on every occasion, in every location, wherever we find ourselves. Because He is all-knowing, His peace is astute, perceptive, and unerring. Because God is faithful, His peace is steadfast.

Philippians 4:7 goes on to describe it this way: "And the peace of God, *which transcends all understanding.*" In other words, the peace of God defies all attempts to describe, analyze, explain, or comprehend it. This is the peace that God Himself possesses within the infinity of His attributes. It's the peace that flows from Him like currents in the ocean and streams in the desert, and it is transcendent.

What can you do to adopt more peace into your life? How can a more peaceful existence impact your anxiety?

*You will keep in perfect peace all who trust
in you, all whose thoughts are fixed on you!*
ISAIAH 26:3 NLT

When it comes to worry and anxiety, there is both a mental and an emotional aspect to them. It is impossible to chart the border between our thoughts and feelings, for they are intertwined like threads in embroidery. But we know from experience how our minds and our hearts bear our concerns differently. Sometimes I have more trouble with a worried mind when my problems barge in and commandeer my thoughts. On other occasions, my nerves are edgy, and I experience feelings of uneasiness, even when my mind struggles to pinpoint the source of my worry. My thoughts give me headaches, and my feelings give me stomachaches.

That's why the God of peace sends two detachments of soldiers to help—one to compose our minds with truth and the other to guard our emotions with trust. As J. B. Phillips translates it: "The peace of God which transcends human understanding, will keep constant guard over your hearts and minds as they rest in Christ Jesus" (Philippians 4:6–7 PHILLIPS).

Do you tend to struggle more with the emotional or physical manifestations of anxiety?

What proactive actions can you take to guard your mind from worry and ease the physical repercussions of anxiety?

"Don't be afraid," he said, "for you are very precious to God. Peace! Be encouraged! Be strong!" As he spoke these words to me, I suddenly felt stronger and said to him, "Please speak to me, my Lord, for you have strengthened me."

DANIEL 10:19 NLT

I had a friend in college named Scott Burlingame. While Scott was serving as a pastor in Columbia, South Carolina, he was diagnosed with cancer, and the news went from bad to worse. Scott's illness proved terminal. During their months on this journey, he and his wife, Joyce, sent prayer updates to friends, and these updates read like journal entries. After Scott's death, she compiled them in a book entitled *Living with Death, Dying with Life.* One of her entries was dated January 17, 2011:

> These are truly hard days. Although Scott can eat just a little, it is not much. I am carefully trying to add new foods, but then find we are back where we started. And drinking enough liquids is also a problem . . . even water is difficult. A mixture of water and Gatorade seems to work the best. He is very weak, and I have to assist him in much of what we took for granted just a few months ago.

I have had to buy him all new clothes twice. . . . The hospice people came yesterday for an initial visit. . . . Right now things are very difficult. I feel as though the hosts of hell have been unleashed against us to bring worry, frustration, confusion, and to attempt to make us doubt all we believe. But, in the words of an old song, "Christ has regarded our helpless estate, and has shed his own blood for our souls!" And in Him we live and move and have our being, and are able to withstand the onslaught of the Enemy. Underneath the anguish is the deep peace of God that passes all understanding.[24]

God's peace isn't the absence of conflict or the nonexistence of problems. It is the Gulf Stream of His grace below the surface levels of life. We lay hold of the transcendent peace of the God of peace, which can stabilize our thoughts and emotions in every situation. That's God's ironclad promise to those who put Philippians 4:4–6 into practice. Verse 7 says, "And the peace of God, which transcends all understanding, will guard your hearts and your minds in Christ Jesus."

How does God's peace stabilize your thoughts and emotions? How can you utilize that peace to control your anxious feelings and thoughts?

Through their faith, the people in days
of old earned a good reputation.

HEBREWS 11:2 NLT

When the writer of the book of Hebrews wanted to encourage his nervous readers to persevere under pressure, he told them, "Now faith is confidence in what we hope for and assurance about what we do not see. This is what the ancients were commended for" (11:1–2). He then listed the examples of Abel, Enoch, Noah, Abraham, and the roll call of Old Testament heroes, who, through faith, conquered kingdoms, shut the mouths of lions, and gained what was promised.

We have two thousand more years of Christian biography to add to that procession, and if we want to strengthen our faith and overcome the armies of anxiety arrayed against us, we need to learn from their examples. If these men and women overcame anxiety, pulled down strongholds, lived boldly for their faith, and gained the reward, so can we. So can our generation.

As we practice rejoicing, gentleness, nearness, prayer, thanksgiving, and meditation, we must add the practice of discipleship. The word *disciple* literally means "learner," and it has to do with following and emulating the teaching and example of another. If we belong to Christ, we're primarily His disciples, but He often uses certain people to spur us on, instruct us, teach us, mentor us, and disciple us in the truths and techniques of our faith. Some of these mentors dwell in yesteryear and cast their shadows over our pathways from afar. Others step right onto our pathways now and come alongside as friends, pastors, counselors, mentors, and teachers. We cannot overcome the anxieties of life without the help of these God-given allies.

How can you add discipleship to your daily routine?

Who are your God-given allies? If you are unsure, prayerfully ask God to identify someone that could serve as a mentor in your life, or read Hebrews 11 to find inspiration from the ancients discussed there.

It is impossible to please God without faith. Anyone who wants to come to him must believe that God exists and that he rewards those who sincerely seek him.

HEBREWS 11:6 NLT

Even at so-called retirement age, I need mentors and advisers more than ever. We seldom evolve from anxious fear to unshakable faith in a day or a week, but we can move from weakness to strength by persevering over time, especially when we let others help us. Earlier in Philippians, Paul encouraged his readers by telling them he was confident "that he who began a good work in you will carry it on to completion until the day of Christ Jesus" (1:6).

That involves process and progress.

The psalmist prayed, "The Lord will perfect that which concerns me; Your mercy, O Lord, endures forever" (Psalm 138:8 NKJV), or, as *The Message* puts it, "Finish what you started in me, God. Your love is eternal—don't quit on me now."

He won't quit on us, and we must not quit either. Month by month, year by year, and decade by decade, we can have greater calmness and composure, growing as sturdy as oaks with the passing of the seasons. Our anxious nerves can learn to relax in

His love, lean on His promises, and trust in His grace. Our peace of mind can overwhelm the baser elements of our personalities.

True, we may have regressions along the way. Everyone who battles some variation of traumatic stress knows how our deepest fears can ignite in an instant when triggered by some word, event, sound, smell, or thought. But Proverbs 24:16 says, "The godly may trip seven times, but they will get up again. But one disaster is enough to overthrow the wicked" (NLT). With the examples of Jesus and His followers through all the ages, we have the resources to keep getting up, continuing on, and gaining ground until the LORD takes us home. When it comes to winning over worry, we never give up.

Is there a specific hardship or season that made you stronger? How did that battle provide you with the knowledge to overcome future traumas?

The LORD is my strength and shield. I trust him with all my heart. He helps me, and my heart is filled with joy. I burst out in songs of thanksgiving.

PSALM 28:7 NLT

Paul wrote Philippians from prison, and he knew the Philippians were anxious about him. They were anxious about themselves amid the hostility of the Roman Empire. Indeed, they were worried about the very survival of Christianity in the Roman world. There was opposition. There was persecution. Their hero had been incarcerated. But throughout the book of Philippians, Paul was calm. He was cheerful. He was optimistic. He was content. He was joyful and excited.

His message: Be like me! Rejoice in the LORD always as I am doing. Let your gentleness be evident to all as I'm trying to do. Don't forget the LORD is near you as He is near me. Learn to do what I am doing—don't be anxious about anything, but in everything by prayer and petition, with thanksgiving, present your requests to God.

In order to bury worry before worry buries you, find someone else with a shovel in their hand, who, by faith, is already putting their anxious cares six feet under. It may be a friend, a grandparent, a writer, a pastor, or a senior saint, someone whose face reflects the peace you need. Get to know them. Learn from them. Talk with them if possible and pray with them. Ask them, "How did you learn to trust the LORD as you do?"

And as you follow their example, you'll begin to notice others—looking to you for their strength in life.

This is the practice of discipleship. Who can you go to and ask, "How did you learn to trust the LORD as you do?"

May God give you more and more grace and peace as you grow in your knowledge of God and Jesus our Lord.

2 PETER 1:2 NLT

When our minds are overtaken with worry, distress, or discouragement, there's only one thing to do. We have to remember. We have to call to mind the truths we need. We have to take control of our thoughts and stop listening to ourselves and start talking to ourselves. We have to preach to ourselves, lecture ourselves, exhort ourselves. In short, we must go on to the next verse in Paul's instruction for a better life—the practice of thinking. Philippians 4:8 says:

> Finally, brothers and sisters, whatever is true, whatever is noble, whatever is right, whatever is pure, whatever is lovely, whatever is admirable—if anything is excellent or praiseworthy—think about such things.

Out of the thirty-two words in that sentence, only one is an action verb, and it's the key word of the verse and the sole imperative—*think*. In terms of his natural personality, I believe the apostle Paul was, to some degree, a bundle of nervous energy, absorbed in his work, and subject to passionate concern. His anxiety in Troas had short-circuited his ministry there, though God had opened great doors in that city. But Paul was a devoted student of the Hebrew Scriptures, and it's clear he searched the books and parchments of the Old Testament for a greater acquisition of the peace of God.

What should you be thinking about? How can the practice of thinking add benefit to your life?

*Think about the things of heaven,
not the things of earth.*

COLOSSIANS 3:2 NLT

If we have anxious thoughts, we'll be anxious people, because what we *think* is the most important thing about us. We *are* what we *think*, and our lives, attitudes, feelings, reactions, results, failures, successes, and personalities are formed by the strands of thought that tie our brain cells together like baling wire. This is so self-evident it's been at the heart of philosophy and religion from the beginning of human civilization.

Even non-Christians know this. The Hindus taught, "Man becomes that of which he thinks." The Buddha said, "The mind is everything: what you think you become." Marcus Aurelius said, "Your life is what your thoughts make it." Descartes wrote: "I think, therefore I am." The nineteenth-century Unitarian preacher William Channing wrote: "All that a man does outwardly is but the expression and completion of his inward thought."[25]

William James laid the foundation for today's motivational movement and positive-thinking literature with these simple words: "The greatest discovery of my generation is that human beings can alter their lives by altering their attitudes of mind."[26]

To calm our anxiety, we must think and we must think rightly, on the right things, at the right time, on the right wavelengths, with our antennae tuned to the frequency of God's truth. We cannot overcome anxiety unless we learn to replace *worried* thoughts with *worthy* thoughts, thoughts that come directly from the mind of the God of peace. That requires thinking on things that are true, noble, lovely, and praiseworthy.

What are you worried about? What worthy thoughts can replace your worries?

Oh, how I love your instructions! I
think about them all day long.

PSALM 119:97 NLT

Thinking is an activity that's fallen on hard times. We're too busy to think, and our minds are congested with noise. It's hard to meditate with our phones clamoring like calliopes, incoming messages arriving like missiles, and headsets blaring like the Tower of Babel.

We don't ride horses into town now. Our work isn't undertaken in quiet fields, disturbed by nothing beyond the murmur of the wind or the distant baying of a dog. We no longer read by the flicker of candlelight or the glow of a fireplace. All that was lost long ago in the Industrial Revolution; now the Information and Technology Revolution instantly delivers the cacophony of the world straight into our eardrums via a billion speakers and earphones. We rush through traffic like salmon bolting upstream for spawning. We're bombarded by noise and besieged by stimuli. Surround sound is a way of life, and lost to us—without true spiritual effort—is the spirit of Isaiah 30:15: "In quietness and confidence shall be your strength" (NKJV). Or Psalm 46:10: "Be still, and know that I am God."

When we learn to take time for thinking, and when we

learn to think in the right way, the benefits come over us like a metamorphosis.

How can you silence the noise and slow down? How can you incorporate these patterns into your daily routine?

In what ways has information and technology aided your spiritual development, and in what ways has it had a negative impact?

But those who obey God's word truly show how completely they love him. This is how we know that we are living in him.

1 JOHN 2:5 NLT

In a sense, the following eight words are a description of God Himself, and of Jesus Christ, who reflects and embodies them perfectly: *true, noble, right, pure, lovely, admirable, excellent,* and *praiseworthy.* According to 2 Corinthians 3:18, we are transformed by contemplating all He is and all He is for us: "And we all, who with unveiled faces contemplate the Lord's glory, are being transformed into his image with ever-increasing glory, which comes from the Lord, who is the Spirit."

These eight words also describe the scope of Scripture, which brings us back to the habits of Bible study, Scripture memory, and contemplative meditation. Romans 8 says, "Those who live according to the flesh have their minds set on what the flesh desires; but those who live in accordance with the Spirit have their minds set on what the Spirit desires. The mind governed by the flesh is death, but the mind governed by the Spirit is life and peace" (vv. 5–6). Notice the word *peace.* It's the same word we find in Philippians 4. When our minds are governed by the Spirit and filled with the Scripture, we're training them to move from panic to peace, from worry to worship, and from anxiety to confident trust. That's why I'm a strong advocate for Scripture memory and meditation.

Equipping yourself with Scriptures will help your mind be trained to move from panic to peace, from worry to worship, and from anxiety to confident trust. Identify three scriptures that will help you make these movements. Recite them each day until you've memorized them.

*Help me understand the meaning
of your commandments, and I will
meditate on your wonderful deeds.*

PSALM 119:27 NLT

As we internalize, visualize, and personalize God's Word, we're transformed into the kind of people He wants us to be. We see things from His perspective. We think increasingly as Jesus does, and our minds are deepened, sharpened, composed, and calmed. J. B. Phillips rendered Romans 12:2 like this: "Don't let the world around you squeeze you into its own mould, but let God re-mould your minds from within" (PHILLIPS).[27]

This strategy saved the life of missionary Geoffrey Bull, a Scottish expatriate who was captured and imprisoned by Chinese communists in Tibet. His possessions, including his Bible, were stripped from him and he was thrown into a series of prisons, where he suffered terribly for three years. In addition to extreme temperatures, scant food, and miserable conditions, Bull was subjected to such mental and psychological torture he feared he would go insane. But he had studied the Bible all his life, so he began to systematically go through Scripture in his mind.

He found it took him about six months to go all the way through the Bible mentally. He started at Genesis, and recalled each incident and story as best he could, first concentrating on the content and then musing on certain points, seeking light in prayer. He continued through the Old Testament, reconstructing the books and chapters as best he could and focusing his thoughts on verses he knew by heart; then into the New Testament and on to Revelation. Then he started over again. He later wrote: "The strength received through this meditation was, I believe, a vital factor in bringing me through, kept by the faith to the very end."[28]

The great thing about internalizing Scripture through memorization and meditation is its power to transform us and even to convert our circumstances and surroundings from anxiety-inducing to praise-producing.

How can (or has) meditation impact(ed) the reduction of your anxiety? Identify a specific instance when your anxiety was greatly impacted by meditation.

Study this Book of Instruction continually.
Meditate on it day and night so you will be
sure to obey everything written in it. Only then
will you prosper and succeed in all you do.

JOSHUA 1:8 NLT

The practice of meditation involves taking a passage of Scripture and *memorizing* it, *visualizing* it, and *personalizing* it. As you do this, your mind is healed by the transforming truth of God's Word and you begin increasingly to think the way God Himself thinks. You begin to look at life from God's point of view. You develop the wisdom from above (James 3:17).[29]

One day while teaching at Liberty University, I had a wonderful conversation about this with my friend Dr. Gary Mathena. He told me of an experience involving his father:

> One of my dad's heroes in the ministry was an African American preacher named Manuel Scott. After hearing Dr. Scott preach one evening, my dad had the opportunity to have breakfast with him the next day. As a young preacher, my dad expressed to Dr. Scott how much he was blessed, encouraged, and inspired by his preaching and the truths he was able to extrapolate out of the Scripture. My dad said, "Dr. Scott, it is so evident that you are a spiritual

man. How does a man become spiritual? How can I learn to preach with the insights and depth with which you preach?"

Manuel Scott thought for a moment and said, "Well, Harold, when you wake up in the morning spend time reading and thinking about the Word of God and then throughout the day meditate and ruminate on the Word of God all day long. And then before you go to sleep at night allow the Word of God to bathe your heart and mind." Then Dr. Scott paused and reached up to put his thumbs under his red suspenders and said, "If you'll do that, then one of these days, you'll just wake up spiritual!"[30]

If you want to worry less and live more, put this into practice immediately: "Whatever is true, whatever is noble, whatever is right, whatever is pure, whatever is lovely, whatever is admirable—if anything is excellent or praiseworthy—think about such things."

Have you reached a spiritual reckoning like Manuel Scott? If you have, how has your overall attitude and anxiety benefited? If not, come up with a plan on how you can incorporate prayer and meditation in your daily routine.

All your words are true; all your
righteous laws are eternal.

PSALM 119:160

Frankly, when I look at the condition of the world, I'm amazed we're not more anxious than we are. And I'm thankful for those who are helping us address these issues genetically, nutritionally, medically, cognitively, and in terms of our lifestyle. I appreciate the doctors, nurses, counselors, therapists, psychologists, psychiatrists, researchers, positive thinkers, pastors, healers, and friends who have helped me through anxious times.

But nothing offers sustained help if we don't have a spiritual foundation based on the LORD Jesus Christ. The core answer to anxiety is a reassuring word from an almighty God. No therapy in the world can match the theology of the Bible. We need help from beyond ourselves and from beyond our worried world. The German humanitarian George Müller spoke for many of us when he said, "Many times when I could have gone insane from worry, I was in peace because my soul believed the truth of [God's] promise."[31]

When do you check in with the LORD about your anxiety? While you're walking, meditating, cooking? Should you check in with Him more frequently?

Who has God brought into your life to help you with your worry or anxiety? Take a moment to thank God for them and for bringing them into your life.

For God has not given us a spirit of fear and
timidity, but of power, love, and self-discipline.
2 TIMOTHY 1:7 NLT

We have to attack anxiety on the basis of spiritual truth, and I believe that's exactly how Paul dealt with his own issues of worry and stress. Knowing him as we do from the pages of the New Testament, we would expect him to fight his affliction with every available spiritual weapon. Whatever his circumstances, whatever his genetic predispositions, whatever his personality, whatever his background, he was a man who strove toward self-improvement. He worked on his spiritual progress and pressed toward the goal for the prize of the high calling of God. He wanted his whole spirit, soul, and body governed by the Holy Spirit.

As Saint Paul prayerfully searched his books and parchments, pouring over the Hebrew Scriptures, I believe he developed a treatment protocol for his anxiety. He was a strategist, after all, and he crafted a game plan for winning over worry. As a physician of the soul, he knew how to wisely self-medicate with biblical truth.

What things are you doing to strive toward self-improvement? How are you working on your spiritual progress? What resources are available to help you?

Meditate on 2 Timothy 1:7 today. At the end of the day, take a moment to reflect on your experience.

And as we live in God, our love grows more perfect. So we will not be afraid on the day of judgment, but we can face him with confidence because we live like Jesus here in this world.

1 JOHN 4:17 NLT

It's easy to be like the mother of my friend Keith Fletcher. As she grew older, she became increasingly cantankerous, difficult, and critical. Her sharp comments made her a bit of a challenge to live with. A couple of months after she passed away, Keith had a dream about her. He dreamed he came downstairs for supper and there she was sitting at the table, the same as always.

"Mom! You're here!" Keith exclaimed. "You're back."

She nodded.

He said, "But you passed away and went to heaven."

She nodded again.

"Mom, if you've been to heaven, you've seen it there and you know what it's like. You can tell us all about heaven. What is it like there? What is heaven really like?"

She shot a glance at him and said curtly, "I didn't like it!"

The question isn't whether we know people like that. It's whether we're like that ourselves more often than we realize. Keith's mother reflects our own natural tendencies. There's a saying that all growth depends upon your activity and willingness to be uncomfortable. You cannot grow if you stay in your comfort zone. If you want to process your feelings and deal with your anxiety, you must be willing to overcome your natural tendencies.

How can you get of your comfort zone and overcome your natural tendencies so you can better deal with your anxiety?

Yes, everything else is worthless when compared with the infinite value of knowing Christ Jesus my Lord. For his sake I have discarded everything else, counting it all as garbage, so that I could gain Christ.

PHILIPPIANS 3:8 NLT

In one of her uplifting poems, Helen Steiner Rice put it like this:

> At the spot God placed you
> Begin at once to do
> Little things that brighten up
> The lives surrounding you.
> For if everybody brightened up
> The spot on which they're standing
> By being more considerate
> And a little less demanding
> This dark old world would very soon
> Eclipse the "Evening Star"
> If everybody brightened up
> The corner where they are.[32]

A gentle spirit not only reduces anxiety; it also reflects Christ. In Matthew 11:29, Jesus spoke of Himself as "gentle and humble in heart," and in Matthew 21:5, others described Him as being "gentle and riding on a . . . colt."

This didn't keep Jesus from speaking plainly when necessary. There were times He condemned hypocrites, denounced cities, and rebuked demons. He occasionally spoke sharply (Matthew 16:23), and just a reproachful glance could reduce a grown man to tears (Luke 22:61–62). But there was never a time when Jesus lost control of Himself or of His words or emotions. The default setting on His personality was one of compassion, love, gentleness, and humility—a willingness to touch and help those with whom He came in contact.

What can you do to create and embrace a gentle spirit for yourself? How do you think your anxiety will benefit from an increased gentleness?

But do this in a gentle and respectful way. Keep your conscience clear. Then if people speak against you, they will be ashamed when they see what a good life you live because you belong to Christ.

1 PETER 3:16 NLT

As I studied the occurrences of the words *gentle* and *gentleness* in the Bible, I also ran into a pragmatic truth. The Bible says we should be gentle because gentleness gets things done. It works. It makes us more efficient, productive, and profitable in the daily business of life. Gentleness not only reduces stress and reflects Christ; it also gets things done.

Proverbs 25:15 discusses this: "Through patience a ruler can be persuaded, and a gentle tongue can break a bone." One of the softest parts of our body is the tongue. God created it with flexibility and motion so we can eat and speak. The most unyielding parts of our body are our bones, which are rigid so we can stand upright.

It takes more energy to react negatively than it does to be gentle. This is true when you're responding to people or yourself. Remember that it is just as important to have a gentle tongue when you're handling your feelings and emotions.

Can you think of a time when you leaned into gentleness in order to get the job done? How did things turn out?

Reflect on a time where it took a lot of energy for you to react negatively. What would have been different had you reacted in a calm spirit?

*I will praise you forever, O God, for what
you have done. I will trust in your good name
in the presence of your faithful people.*

PSALM 52:9 NLT

When I forget God's presence, I'm living in a state of denial, pretense, and error. When I practice His presence, I'm dealing with reality, and reality fosters peace.

I read in the newspaper what happened to Blossie Anderson, a spunky eighty-five-year-old great-grandmother who decided to go fishing along the Saluda River near Greenville, South Carolina. When her sixty-two-year-old son, Louis, tried to dissuade her, she said, "I had you; you didn't have me."

Trudging into the snake-infested swamp with her fishing pole, she fell, struggled back to her feet, became disoriented, and waded through the area in the wrong direction. She finally sat down exhausted, hoping someone would come for her. "I wasn't afraid," she said, "I knew the Lord was with me, and I knew the Lord would bring help, so I just waited."

Rescuers mounted an extensive search, but they were looking on the wrong side of the river. The elderly woman just sat where she was, waiting and reminding herself that God was near her.

Four days later a rescuer thrashing around the area heard an elderly voice calling, "Hey, mister." The rescuer said, "Granny! How are you?"

"Lord have mercy," she replied, "I've been here for four days without anything to eat." She was taken to Greenville General Hospital where she was treated for exhaustion and dehydration and released. She later told reporters, "I slept at night and rested during the day. I wasn't cold, and I wasn't afraid of them snakes. God was with me, keeping me warm and keeping the snakes' jaws shut."[33]

God's very real presence sustained her. Every believer from biblical times until today has experienced disorienting days—but never a day when the LORD wasn't with us, keeping us warm and keeping the snakes' jaws shut.

Your experience may not be as dramatic, but think of a time when you felt lost and had to wait for help. Did you feel the LORD's nearness? How did the LORD provide for you during this time?

Let us go right into the presence of God with sincere hearts fully trusting him. For our guilty consciences have been sprinkled with Christ's blood to make us clean, and our bodies have been washed with pure water.

HEBREWS 10:22 NLT

During the Great Awakening of 1857–1858, according to historian Wesley Duewel, the canopy of the presence of the Holy Spirit "seemed to hang like an invisible cloud over many parts of the United States, especially over the eastern seaboard. At times this cloud of God's presence even seemed to extend out to sea. Those on ships approaching the east coast at times felt a solemn, holy influence, even one hundred miles away. . . . Revival began aboard one ship before it reached the coast. People on board began to feel the presence of God and a sense of their own sinfulness. The Holy Spirit convicted them, and they began to pray."[34]

In some revivals, people sensed the presence of God so powerfully they "felt as if the Lord had breathed upon them." And according to one eyewitness during the 1906 Welsh revival, "a sense of the Lord's presence was everywhere. It pervaded, nay, it created the spiritual atmosphere. It mattered not where one went, the consciousness of the reality and nearness of God followed . . . in the homes, on the streets, in the mines and factories, in the schools." Observers described how "the cloud of God's presence hung low over much of Wales for months."[35]

I've never had an experience quite as dramatic as those, but I am learning to recognize God's abiding presence by faith. As wonderful as these revival accounts are, they were momentary reminders of an enduring truth—the LORD is within us, around us, shielding, hovering over, accompanying, abiding with, and attending to us at all times, whether we can physically sense His presence or not. We walk by faith, not by feelings, but that doesn't diminish the reality of His nearness. He has so often reassured us of His presence; how could we doubt Him?

When was the last time the LORD reassured you of His presence? Where were you? How was your faith reaffirmed?

Rejoice in our confident hope. Be patient
in trouble, and keep on praying.

ROMANS 12:12 NLT

Prayer is the buffer zone of the soul, where fear is repulsed and where grace and guidance are gained. This is the process described in Philippians 4:6: "Do not be anxious about anything, but in every situation, by prayer and petition, with thanksgiving, present your requests to God."

Perhaps Paul had drawn his principle from Psalm 37: "Do not fret. . . . Trust in the LORD. . . . Take delight in the LORD. . . . Commit your way to the LORD. . . . Be still before the LORD and wait patiently for him; do not fret. . . . Do not fret—it leads only to evil" (vv. 1, 3–5, 7–8).

Perhaps he was thinking of Christ's words in Matthew 6: "Pray to your Father, who is unseen. . . . Pray: 'Our Father in heaven.' . . . Therefore I tell you, do not worry. . . . Why do you worry? . . . So do not worry. . . . Therefore do not worry" (vv. 6, 9, 25, 28, 31, 34).

Somehow the apostle Paul squeezed, condensed, and compressed two great chapters of the Bible—Psalm 37 and Matthew 6—into one incredible verse—Philippians 4:6—and every phrase of this verse is a wonder of psychology and spirituality.

What are some small things you can do every day to embrace Philippians 4:6 as a motto for your life?

If prayer is the "buffer zone" of the soul, are you doing enough to keep this zone strong? How can you make more time for prayer in your daily routine?

*I prayed to the LORD, and he answered
me. He freed me from all my fears.*

PSALM 34:4 NLT

Paul wrote the book of Philippians from jail, where he had faced a host of discomforting circumstances. He talked about what had happened to him, what might happen to him, and about the circumstances and situations that had come unwelcomed into his life:

- In Philippians 1:12, he said, "I want you to know, brothers and sisters, that what has happened to me . . ."
- In verse 19, he again talked about "what has happened to me."
- In verse 27, he told them, "Whatever happens, conduct yourselves in a manner worthy of the gospel."
- In Philippians 2:23, he said he would send Timothy to them, "as soon as I see how things go."
- In Philippians 4:6, he used the phrase "in every situation."
- In verse 11, he spoke of his ability to remain composed, "whatever the circumstances."

- In verse 12, he said, "I have learned the secret of being content in any and every situation."

All these phrases indicate things were happening to Paul outside his control. But rather than worrying about them, he had learned he could bring them to the LORD and pray about every one of them, knowing that under God's providential control each situation would, in the final analysis, turn in a good-ward and in a Godward direction. The LORD's providential ordering of all things for the good of His children is just as certain as the resurrection of Christ from the grave on the third day.

What is causing you to be worried? Is there something triggering your anxiety? Make a commitment to give providential control to the LORD. How does this Godward direction help ease your worries and reduce your anxiety?

Notes

1. Samuel Bradburn, *Select Letters: Chiefly on Personal Religion, by the Rev. John Wesley* (New York: T. Mason and G. Lane, 1838), 14.

2. Joy Ridderhof, *Are You Rejoicing?* (Los Angeles, CA: Global Recordings Network, 1984), entry for day 1.

3. Katie Hoffman, *A Life of Joy* (n.p.: Ano Klesis Publishing, 2006), 150–51.

4. Harry Bollback, *Our Incredible Journey* (Schroon Lake NY: Word of Life Fellowship, 2011),181.

5. Monica Cantilero, "Married for 75 Years Without a Single Fight," Christian Today, August 11, 2015, www.christiantoday.com/article/married.for.75.years. without.a.single.fight.us.christian.couple.gets.medias. attention/61583.htm.

6. Jessica Bringe, "Area Couple Celebrates 75 Years of Marriage," *WEAU News*, www.weau.com/home/headlines/Area-couple-celebrates-75-years-of-marriage-320981951.html.

7. Fred Smith Sr., *Breakfast with Fred* (Ventura, CA: Regal, 2007), 48–49.

8. Donna Kincheloe, *I Never Walk the Halls Alone* (Nashville, TN: ACW Press, 2007), 72–74.

9. Kincheloe, *I Never Walk the Halls Alone*, 72–74.

10. Phil Mason, *Napoleon's Hemorrhoids: And Other Small Events That Changed the World* (New York: Skyhorse Publishing, 2009), 31.

11. Based on a conversation with Rocky Forshey; used with permission.

12. John Wooden, *The Essential Wooden* (New York: McGraw-Hill, 2007), 8–9.

13. Wooden, *The Essential Wooden*, 8–9.

14. Wooden, 11.

15. Quoted by Harold C. Lyon in *Tenderness Is Strength: From Machismo to Manhood* (New York: Harper & Row, 1977), 7.

16. Maxwell Cornelius, "Sometime We'll Understand," hymn published in 1891.

17. William M. Anderson, *The Faith That Satisfies* (New York: Loizeaux Brothers, 1948), 165.

18. Adapted from numerous newspaper articles, including "Fliers' Prayers Answered," *NZ Herald*, May 20, 2008, www.nzherald.co.nz/nz/news/article.cfm?c_id=1&objectid=10511547; and "Pilot of 'Doomed' Aircraft Claims That His Passenger's Prayers Helped the Pair Land Safely," *Daily Mail*, May 21, 2008, www.dailymail.co.uk/news/article-1020917/Pilot-doomed-aircraft-claims-passengers-prayers-helped-pair-land-safely.html; and other similar articles.

19. Robert A. Emmons, *Thanks! How Practicing Gratitude Can Make You Happier* (Boston: Houghton Mifflin Company, 2007), 11.

20. Emmons, *Thanks! How Practicing Gratitude*, 22.

21. Emmons, 3.

22. Emmons, 11.

23. I recall hearing Vance Havner use a similar phrase years ago.

24. Joyce Burlingame, *Living with Death, Dying with Life* (Bloomington, IN: Westbow, 2015), 130–31.

25. Lillian Eichler Watson, *Light from Many Lamps* (New York: Simon and Schuster, 1951), 169–74.

26. Arthur L. Young, "Attitude and Altitude," *New Outlook: Volume 8, Number 11*, November, 1955, 42.

27. Some of this material is adapted from my book *Reclaiming the Lost Art of Biblical Meditation* (Nashville: HarperCollins, 2016), where the reader can find these ideas expanded into a variety of practical applications.

28. Geoffrey T. Bull, *When Iron Gates Yield* (Chicago: Moody Press), passim.

29. These insights came from attending an Institute of Basic Youth Conflicts seminar in the 1970s.

30. As told to Dr. Gary Mathena, director of practica for the School of Music at Liberty University, by his father, Dr. Harold Mathena.

31. George Müller, *The Autobiography of George Müller* (New Kensington, PA: Whitaker House, 1984), 155.

32. Helen Steiner Rice, *Poems of Faith* (Carmel, NY: Guideposts, 1981), 33–34.

33. This story appeared in numerous newspapers in September 1981, including *Gaffney Ledger*, September 4, 1981; *Schenectady Gazette*, September 4, 1981; *Daytona Beach Morning Journal*, September 4, 1981; and in Steve Petrone, "Woman, 85, Proves She's Tough-As-Nails After Her 4 Days in Horror Swamp," *Weekly World News*, September 29, 1981.

34. Wesley Duewel, *Revival Fire* (Grand Rapids: Zondervan, 1995), 134.

35. Duewel, *Revival Fire*, 141, 183–84.

ROBERT J. MORGAN

Bestselling Author of *The Red Sea Rules* and *The Strength You Need*

calm
YOUR ANXIETY

winning the fight against worry

AVAILABLE WHEREVER BOOKS ARE SOLD

THE
Robert J. Morgan
PODCAST

If you've ever heard or read Robert J. Morgan, you know to expect sound Bible teaching and a healthy dose of Christian history and hymnity.

Scan the QR code below to enjoy weekly free episodes of The Robert J. Morgan Podcast.

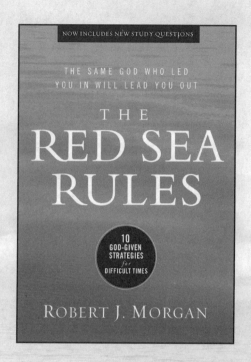

NOW INCLUDES NEW STUDY QUESTIONS

THE SAME GOD WHO LED
YOU IN WILL LEAD YOU OUT

THE
RED SEA
RULES

10
GOD-GIVEN
STRATEGIES
for
DIFFICULT TIMES

ROBERT J. MORGAN

AVAILABLE WHEREVER BOOKS ARE SOLD